The Wealthy Recession

Investing during a recession, an introduction.

By Ian. L Bradshaw

PROLOGUE

The world of investing is filled with twists and turns, highs and lows, and a fair share of uncertainty. But when a recession hits, the game changes. Suddenly, everything investors once knew is thrown out the window, and they are left with a whole new set of challenges to navigate.

INTRO

Looking back at past recessions, it's clear that there have been both mistakes and successes when it comes to investing. One common mistake has been panic selling - when investors sell off their stocks in a frenzy, leading to a further drop in prices. This was seen during the Great Recession of 2008, when many investors panicked and sold off their stocks at low prices, only to miss out on the eventual market rebound.

On the other hand, there have been success stories as well. Some investors have taken advantage of low stock prices during recessions to buy in at a discount, and then reaped the benefits when the market eventually recovered. One notable example of this was Warren Buffett, who invested heavily in stocks during the 2008 recession, and saw his investments pay off handsomely in the years that followed.

Looking ahead, there are always possibilities for both mistakes and successes in recession investing. One potential mistake could be overreacting to short-term market fluctuations, rather than focusing on long-term fundamentals. On the other hand, a potential success could be finding undervalued companies that are poised for growth, even during tough economic times.

Real-life examples of these possibilities abound. For instance, during the COVID-19 pandemic, some investors panicked and sold off their stocks, while others saw it as an opportunity to buy in at a discount. Similarly, some investors focused on short-term market fluctuations, while others focused on long-term fundamentals and identified companies that were well-positioned for growth, such as those in the technology and healthcare sectors.

In the pages that follow, we will explore these mistakes and successes in greater detail, and provide strategies and insights to help investors make informed decisions during times of economic uncertainty.

CHAPTER 1. EMERGENCY FUNDS:

An emergency fund is an essential component of any financial plan, and it becomes even more critical during a recession. Here are some key things to keep in mind when building and managing your emergency fund during a recession.

1.1. Determine how much you need:
The first step in building an emergency fund is to determine how much you need to save. Experts recommend having at least 3-6 months' worth of living expenses saved in an emergency fund. However, during a recession, it may be wise to have more than that, up to 12 months' worth of expenses, to provide a greater safety net.

Determining how much money you need for an emergency fund during a recession is an important part of financial planning. An emergency fund is a sum of money that you set aside for unexpected expenses or emergencies, such as a job loss or a medical emergency. The goal of an emergency fund is to provide a financial safety net that can help you avoid taking on debt or dipping into other savings accounts.

Here are the steps to determine how much money you need for an emergency fund during a recession:

S1. Calculate your monthly expenses: The first step is to determine your monthly expenses. This includes all of your fixed expenses, such as rent or mortgage payments, utilities, and insurance, as well as your variable expenses, such as groceries, entertainment, and travel. Be sure to include all of your expenses to get an accurate estimate.

S2. - Consider your job security: During a recession, job security may be more uncertain. If you are worried about a potential job loss, you may want to consider increasing your emergency fund to cover a longer period of time.

S3. - Assess your risk tolerance: Your risk tolerance is your ability to handle financial risk. If you have a low risk tolerance, you may want to consider increasing your emergency fund to provide a greater sense of security.

S4. - Determine your target emergency fund amount: Based on your monthly expenses, job security, and risk tolerance, you can determine your target emergency fund amount. Financial experts typically recommend having three to six months of living expenses in your emergency fund, but during a recession, you may want to consider increasing this amount to cover a longer period of time.

During a recession, having a solid emergency fund can provide peace of mind and financial stability. By following these steps, you can determine how much money you need for an emergency fund and start saving to protect yourself from unexpected expenses or emergencies.

1.2. Save aggressively:
Once you've determined how much you need to save, it's important to save aggressively. Set a goal for how much you want to save each month, and make it a priority. Look for ways to cut back on expenses and increase your income, such as taking on a side job or selling items you no longer need.

1.3. Keep your emergency fund separate:
It's important to keep your emergency fund separate from your regular checking or savings account. This can help you avoid the temptation to dip into it for non-emergency expenses. Consider opening a high-yield savings account or money market account specifically for your emergency fund.

1.4. Consider a tiered approach:
Depending on your financial situation, you may want to consider a tiered approach to your emergency fund. A tiered approach to an emergency fund during a recession involves dividing your emergency fund into different tiers, each with a different purpose and level of accessibility. Here are some examples of the tiers that you may want to consider:

Tier 1:
Immediate access emergency fund

This tier is designed to provide immediate access to cash in case of a financial emergency. It should be highly liquid and easily accessible, such as a traditional savings or checking account. This tier should ideally be able to cover at least three to six months of living expenses.

Example: If you lose your job during a recession, having an immediate access emergency fund can help cover your living expenses while you look for a new job.

Tier 2:
High-yield savings account

This tier is designed to provide higher returns than a traditional savings account, while still maintaining a relatively high level of liquidity. A high-yield savings account may offer a higher interest rate than a traditional savings account and is typically FDIC-insured up to $250,000.

Example: You may want to keep a portion of your emergency fund in a high-yield savings account to earn higher interest while still having quick access to cash in case of an emergency.

Tier 3:
Money market account or short-term CD

This tier is designed to provide slightly higher returns than a high-yield savings account, but with a slightly lower level of liquidity. A money market account or short-term certificate of deposit (CD) may offer higher interest rates than a traditional savings account or high-yield savings account but may require a minimum balance or a penalty for early withdrawal.

Example: You may want to keep a portion of your emergency fund in a money market account or short-term CD to earn higher interest than a traditional savings account or high-yield savings account, while still having relatively quick access to cash in case of an emergency.

Tier 4:
Long-term investments

This tier is designed to provide higher returns than a traditional savings account or high-yield savings account but with lower liquidity and potentially higher risks. Long-term investments such as stocks, mutual funds, or exchange-traded funds (ETFs) may offer higher returns over the long term, but may also be subject to market fluctuations and may not be as easily accessible in case of an emergency.

Example: You may want to keep a portion of your emergency fund in long-term investments to potentially earn higher returns over the long term, but you should be prepared to accept some risk and understand that these investments may not be as easily accessible in case of an emergency.

A tiered approach to an emergency fund during a recession can help you tailor your approach to your specific financial situation and provide flexibility, maximize returns, avoid penalties, and provide peace of mind. By dividing your emergency fund into different tiers, you can protect yourself from unexpected financial setbacks while still earning a reasonable return on your investment.

1.5. Re-evaluate your expenses:
During a recession, it's important to re-evaluate your expenses and look for ways to cut back. This can help you stretch your emergency fund further and reduce the amount you need to save. Look for areas where you can trim expenses, such as eating out less, canceling subscription services, or downsizing your home or car.

1.6. Use your emergency fund wisely:
If you do need to use your emergency fund during a recession, use it wisely. Focus on covering essential expenses such as rent/mortgage, utilities, and food. Avoid using your emergency fund for discretionary expenses such as entertainment or travel.

In summary, an emergency fund is a crucial component of your financial plan during a recession. By determining how much you need, saving aggressively, keeping your emergency fund separate, considering a tiered approach, re-evaluating your expenses, and using your emergency fund wisely, you can ensure that you're prepared for any unexpected financial challenges that may arise.

CHAPTER 2. QUALITY INVESTMENTS

Quality investments are a key strategy for investors during a recession. These are investments that have a strong track record of performance, a solid balance sheet, and a high level of stability. Here are some key things to keep in mind when looking for quality investments during a recession.

2.1. Look for stocks that pay dividends:
During a recession, it's important to look for stocks that pay dividends. Dividend-paying stocks can provide a steady stream of income during a downturn, even if the stock price declines. Additionally, companies that pay dividends tend to be more stable and well-established.

A dividend is a payment made by a company to its shareholders, typically in the form of cash or additional shares of stock. Not all stocks pay dividends, but those that do are often viewed as a good investment during a recession because they provide a steady source of income for investors even when the stock market is struggling.

During a recession, companies may cut back on investments or reduce their workforce, which can lead to a decline in stock prices. However, companies that pay dividends are generally more established and financially stable, which can make them a more reliable investment option. Even if their stock price declines during a recession, investors can still receive a regular dividend payment, which can help offset some of the losses.

There are different ways to obtain stocks with dividends. One option is to purchase individual stocks through a brokerage account. Many publicly traded companies, particularly those in mature industries such as utilities, telecommunications, and consumer goods, pay regular dividends to their shareholders. Investors can research these companies to identify those that have a history of paying steady dividends and have the potential for future growth.

Another option is to invest in dividend-paying exchange-traded funds (ETFs) or mutual funds. These funds invest in a diversified portfolio of dividend-paying stocks, which can help reduce the risks associated with investing in individual stocks.

Examples of successful stocks with dividends include:

Procter & Gamble (PG):
This consumer goods company has a long history of paying dividends and has increased its dividend payout every year for more than six decades.

Coca-Cola (KO):
This beverage company has paid consistent dividends for more than a century and has increased its dividend payout for 59 consecutive years.

Johnson & Johnson (JNJ):

This healthcare company has paid dividends for more than 50 years and has increased its dividend payout for 58 consecutive years.

Verizon (VZ):
This telecommunications company has paid steady dividends for more than three decades and has increased its dividend payout for 14 consecutive years.

Overall, investing in stocks with dividends can provide investors with a steady source of income during a recession while also offering the potential for long-term growth. However, as with any investment, it's important to conduct thorough research and carefully evaluate the risks before making a decision.

2.2. Focus on companies with strong balance sheets:

Investing in companies with strong balance sheets can be a sound strategy during a recession. A strong balance sheet typically means a company has a solid financial foundation, with more assets than liabilities and a manageable level of debt. Such companies are typically better positioned to weather economic downturns because they have more financial resources available to them.

During a recession, companies with weak balance sheets may struggle to meet their debt obligations, which can lead to bankruptcy or other financial distress. In contrast, companies with strong balance sheets may be able to take advantage of opportunities presented by a recession, such as acquiring distressed assets or expanding market share.

Investors can find companies with strong balance sheets by looking at a few key financial ratios. Some of the most important ones to consider include:

- Current Ratio: This measures a company's ability to meet its short-term obligations by dividing its current assets (cash, accounts receivable, inventory, etc.) by its current liabilities (accounts payable, accrued expenses, short-term debt, etc.). A current ratio of 2 or higher is generally considered strong.

- Debt-to-Equity Ratio: This measures a company's level of debt relative to its equity (the value of its assets minus its liabilities). A lower debt-to-equity ratio indicates a company has less debt relative to its equity and may be better positioned to handle economic downturns.

- Interest Coverage Ratio: This measures a company's ability to pay its interest expenses on its debt by dividing its earnings before interest and taxes (EBIT) by its interest expenses. A higher interest coverage ratio indicates a company has more earnings available to cover its interest expenses and may be less likely to default on its debt.

- Return on Equity (ROE): This measures a company's profitability by dividing its net income by its equity. A higher ROE indicates a company is generating more profit relative to its equity and may be more financially stable.

Investors can find this financial data on various financial websites such as Yahoo Finance, Google Finance, or Morningstar. They can also access financial reports, such as 10-K filings, from the company's website or the Securities and Exchange Commission's (SEC) EDGAR database.

Overall, investing in companies with strong balance sheets can be a smart strategy during a recession. While no investment is completely risk-free, companies with strong balance sheets are generally more financially stable and better positioned to weather economic downturns than those with weaker financials.

2.3. Consider defensive sectors:
During a recession, certain sectors of the economy tend to hold up better than others. The defensive sector is a term used to describe a group of industries that are considered to be less sensitive to changes in the overall economy, and therefore, may be more stable during periods of economic downturns. These industries are known for providing essential goods and services that are in demand, regardless of economic conditions, such as healthcare, utilities, and consumer staples.

Investing in the defensive sector during a recession can be beneficial for several reasons. Firstly, these industries tend to have more stable earnings and cash flows, which can provide a buffer against economic volatility. Secondly, defensive stocks often pay dividends, which can provide a source of income during a recession when other sources of income, such as job earnings, may be less certain. Lastly, these industries tend to have lower levels of debt, which can make them more resilient during periods of economic stress.

Some examples of companies in the defensive sector include:

Johnson & Johnson (JNJ):
A healthcare company that produces pharmaceuticals, medical devices, and consumer health products. The demand for healthcare products and services tends to be less cyclical than other industries, making it a defensive sector.

Procter & Gamble (PG):
A consumer goods company that produces products such as household cleaning supplies, personal care products, and baby products. Consumer staples like these are essential products that people tend to continue buying regardless of economic conditions.

PepsiCo (PEP):
A beverage and snack food company that is considered a consumer staple. The demand for these products tends to be stable regardless of economic conditions, making them a defensive sector.

Duke Energy (DUK):
A utility company that provides electricity and gas services. Utilities are often considered a defensive sector due to their essential nature and stable earnings.

Overall, investing in the defensive sector during a recession can be a smart strategy for investors looking for stability and potential income during times of economic uncertainty.

2.4. Look for companies with a history of resilience:

During a recession, it's important to look for companies that have a history of resilience. These are companies that have weathered previous economic downturns and come out stronger on the other side. Look for companies that have a strong competitive advantage, a loyal customer base, and a solid track record of innovation.

2.5. Consider real estate investments with strong growth potential:

Real estate investments can be a good way to diversify your portfolio and can offer strong growth potential during a recession, as the value of properties may increase over time despite temporary market downturns. The key to success is investing in properties with strong fundamentals, such as a desirable location, good condition, and high rental demand.

One area with potential for growth during a recession is residential real estate in desirable locations. In some cases, people may choose to rent rather than purchase a home during an economic downturn, which can drive up demand for rental properties. Additionally, properties in popular vacation or tourist destinations may be more resilient to economic downturns, as people may still choose to travel and rent vacation homes.

Another area with potential for growth during a recession is commercial real estate, particularly in industries that are more recession-resistant. For example, properties leased to medical offices, government agencies, or essential businesses such as grocery stores or pharmacies may continue to generate rental income during a recession.

One historical example of a successful real estate investment during a recession is the purchase of distressed properties during the 2008 financial crisis. Investors who had the financial means to buy foreclosed homes or other distressed properties at discounted prices were able to generate significant returns as the market recovered in the years that followed.

To start investing in real estate, there are several options to consider:

- Direct ownership: This involves purchasing a property outright and managing it yourself. This option requires a significant upfront investment and ongoing time and effort to manage the property.

- Real estate investment trusts (REITs): This is a type of investment fund that owns and manages income-generating real estate properties. Investors can buy shares of a REIT on a stock exchange, providing exposure to real estate without the hassle of managing a property.

- Real estate crowdfunding: This involves investing in a real estate project with a group of other investors. This option may require a lower upfront investment but can still provide exposure to real estate investments.

- Real estate partnerships: This involves partnering with another investor or group of investors to purchase and manage a property together. This option can provide access to larger, more expensive properties that may be out of reach for individual investors.

Before investing in real estate, it's important to do thorough research, assess the risks and potential returns, and consult with a financial advisor or real estate professional to ensure it aligns with your financial goals and risk tolerance.

In summary, quality investments can help investors weather a recession and come out stronger on the other side. Look for stocks that pay dividends, focus on companies with strong balance sheets, consider defensive sectors, look for companies with a history of resilience, and consider real estate investments with strong growth potential. By focusing on quality investments, you can help mitigate risk and position yourself for long-term success.

CHAPTER 3. DOLLAR-COST AVERAGING

Dollar-cost averaging is an investment strategy that involves investing a fixed amount of money at regular intervals over a period of time, regardless of market conditions. This strategy can be particularly useful during a recession when the market is volatile and investors may be hesitant to invest large amounts of money all at once. Here are some key things to keep in mind when using dollar-cost averaging during a recession.

3.1. Stay disciplined:
Dollar-cost averaging requires discipline and consistency. It's important to stick to your investment plan and continue to invest the same amount of money at regular intervals, regardless of market conditions. This can be challenging during a recession when market fluctuations can be unsettling. However, staying disciplined can help you avoid making emotional decisions that could harm your long-term investment goals.

3.2. Take advantage of market dips:
Taking advantage of market dips during a recession with dollar-cost averaging can be a smart investment strategy for long-term investors. Dollar-cost averaging is a technique that involves investing a fixed amount of money into a specific investment at regular intervals,

regardless of market conditions. This strategy can help you take advantage of market dips and potentially buy more shares of a particular investment when prices are lower.

Here are the steps to take advantage of market dips during a recession with dollar-cost averaging:

Determine your investment goals and risk tolerance: Before you start investing, it's important to determine your investment goals and risk tolerance. Are you investing for retirement, a future purchase, or another long-term goal? How much risk are you comfortable taking on? This will help you determine the types of investments that are appropriate for you.

Choose your investments:
Once you have determined your investment goals and risk tolerance, you can choose your investments. You may want to consider investing in low-cost index funds or exchange-traded funds (ETFs) that track broad market indexes, such as the S&P 500. These types of investments can provide diversification and exposure to a variety of companies.

Set up automatic investments:
To take advantage of market dips with dollar-cost averaging, set up automatic investments at regular intervals. For example, you may want to invest $500 every month into your chosen investment. This way, you will be investing the same amount of money regardless of market conditions.

Stay disciplined:
It's important to stay disciplined and stick to your investment plan, even during periods of market volatility. Avoid making emotional decisions based on short-term market movements and focus on your long-term investment goals.

Rebalance your portfolio:
Over time, your portfolio may become unbalanced due to market fluctuations. To maintain a diversified portfolio, consider rebalancing your investments at regular intervals, such as once a year. This involves selling some investments and buying others to maintain your desired asset allocation.

Taking advantage of market dips during a recession with dollar-cost averaging can help you build a diversified investment portfolio and potentially buy more shares of your chosen investments when prices are lower.

3.3. Spread out your risk:
Dollar-cost averaging can help you spread out your investment risk over time. By investing a fixed amount of money at regular intervals, you'll be buying shares at various price points. This can help you avoid investing all your money at a single point in time when prices may be high.

3.4. Stick to quality investments:
It's important to stick to quality investments when using dollar-cost averaging during a recession. Look for companies with strong balance sheets, a history of

profitability, and a track record of resilience during economic downturns. These companies are more likely to weather the storm and come out stronger on the other side.

3.5. Have a long-term perspective:
Dollar-cost averaging is a long-term investment strategy. It's important to have a long-term perspective and focus on your investment goals rather than short-term market fluctuations. By sticking to your investment plan and continuing to invest over time, you'll be better positioned to achieve your long-term financial goals.

In summary, dollar-cost averaging can be a useful investment strategy during a recession. By staying disciplined, taking advantage of market dips, spreading out your risk, sticking to quality investments, and having a long-term perspective, you can position yourself for long-term investment success.

CHAPTER 4. INVESTMENT DIVERSIFICATION

Investment diversification is a key strategy for investors during a recession. By diversifying your investments across different asset classes, industries, and geographies, you can help mitigate risk and protect your portfolio during periods of economic uncertainty. Here are some key things to keep in mind when diversifying your investments during a recession.

4.1. Spread your investments across asset classes: Spreading your investments across asset classes is a technique known as asset allocation, and it can be an effective way to manage risk and potentially improve returns during a recession. By spreading your investments across different types of assets, such as stocks, bonds, and real estate, you can reduce your exposure to any one asset class and increase your chances of earning positive returns during periods of market volatility.

Here are the benefits and steps to spread your investments across asset classes during a recession:

Benefits:

Reduce risk:
Spreading your investments across different asset classes can reduce your exposure to any one asset

class and lower your overall portfolio risk.

Diversify your portfolio:
Investing in different asset classes can help diversify your portfolio, potentially improving your chances of earning positive returns during a recession.

Manage risk and returns:
By allocating your investments across different asset classes, you can manage your portfolio's risk and return potential based on your investment goals and risk tolerance.

Steps:

Determine your investment goals and risk tolerance:
Before you begin investing, it's important to determine your investment goals and risk tolerance. Are you investing for long-term growth, income, or a combination of both? How much risk are you comfortable taking on? This will help you determine the appropriate asset allocation for your portfolio.

Choose your asset classes:
Once you have determined your investment goals and risk tolerance, you can choose your asset classes. Some common asset classes include stocks, bonds, real estate, and commodities. Each asset class has different risk and return characteristics, so it's important to choose a mix of assets that align with your investment goals and risk tolerance.

Allocate your investments:

Once you have chosen your asset classes, you can allocate your investments across them.

There are various methods for allocating investments during a recession, and the optimal approach will depend on your investment goals, risk tolerance, and market conditions. Here are some common methods for allocating investments during a recession:

- Strategic Asset Allocation: Strategic asset allocation involves setting target allocations for different asset classes based on your investment goals, risk tolerance, and market conditions. For example, a strategic asset allocation may involve allocating 60% of your portfolio to stocks, 30% to bonds, and 10% to alternative investments such as real estate or commodities. This approach typically involves rebalancing your portfolio on a regular basis to maintain your target allocations.

- Tactical Asset Allocation:
  Tactical asset allocation involves making short-term adjustments to your portfolio based on market conditions and other factors. For example, if you believe that stocks are undervalued during a recession, you may increase your allocation to stocks and decrease your allocation to bonds. This approach requires active management and may involve more frequent trading than strategic asset allocation.

- Dynamic Asset Allocation:
  Dynamic asset allocation involves adjusting your

portfolio allocations based on quantitative models or other systematic methods. For example, a dynamic asset allocation strategy may involve adjusting your portfolio based on signals such as moving averages, relative strength, or economic indicators. This approach may involve less subjectivity than tactical asset allocation but requires sophisticated modeling and analysis.

- Risk Parity:
Risk parity involves allocating your portfolio based on the risk contribution of each asset class rather than the market value. For example, if stocks are more volatile than bonds, a risk parity approach may allocate more to bonds to balance the risk across the portfolio. This approach can help manage risk but requires careful analysis of each asset class's risk characteristics.

- Factor Investing:
Factor investing involves targeting specific investment factors such as value, growth, momentum, or quality. For example, during a recession, you may focus on value stocks that are undervalued relative to their fundamentals. This approach can help you capture specific risk premia and may offer better risk-adjusted returns than a broad-based allocation.

- The "rule of 100,":
This involves subtracting your age from 100 to

determine the percentage of your portfolio that should be invested in stocks. For example, if you are 40 years old, you would invest 60% of your portfolio in stocks and 40% in bonds.

When allocating investments during a recession, it's important to consider the trade-offs between risk and return, as well as your long-term investment goals.

Monitor and adjust your portfolio. Over time, your portfolio may become unbalanced due to market fluctuations. To maintain a diversified portfolio, it's important to monitor your investments regularly and rebalance as needed. This involves selling some investments and buying others to maintain your desired asset allocation.

spreading your investments across asset classes can be an effective way to manage risk and potentially improve returns during a recession. By diversifying your portfolio and managing your risk and return potential based on your investment goals and risk tolerance, you can build a portfolio that aligns with your long-term investment strategy.

4.2. Invest in different industries:
Investing in a range of different industries during a recession is a sound investment strategy for several reasons:

Diversification:
By investing in a range of different industries, you can

spread your risk and reduce the impact of any single industry's downturn on your overall portfolio. Different industries tend to perform differently during a recession, so by investing in a range of industries, you can protect your portfolio from the negative effects of a single industry's decline.

Opportunity:
During a recession, some industries may be hit harder than others, while others may actually perform better. By investing in a range of industries, you can take advantage of opportunities in industries that may be undervalued or have the potential for growth despite the economic downturn.

Long-term growth potential:
While some industries may struggle during a recession, others may continue to experience growth or even outperform the broader market. By investing in a range of industries, you can position yourself to benefit from the long-term growth potential of different sectors, even if they experience short-term setbacks.

Hedging against inflation:
During a recession, governments often implement monetary policies such as low-interest rates or quantitative easing to stimulate the economy. This can lead to inflation, which can erode the value of your investments. By investing in a range of different industries, you can hedge against inflation and protect your portfolio from the effects of rising prices.

Opportunity for income:

Some industries, such as utilities, healthcare, and consumer staples, tend to be less affected by economic downturns and can provide steady income through dividends. By investing in a range of industries, you can diversify your income stream and potentially benefit from the stable dividends of these industries.

Investing in a range of different industries during a recession can provide diversification, opportunities, long-term growth potential, inflation protection, and income. By spreading your risk and taking advantage of opportunities across different sectors, you can position yourself for success even during challenging economic times..

4.3. Consider geographic diversification:
Geographic diversification is an investment strategy that involves spreading your investments across different regions of the world. During a recession, geographic diversification can be particularly beneficial for several reasons:

Risk Management:
Different regions of the world may be impacted differently by a recession. By investing in multiple regions, you can reduce the risk of being overly exposed to any one region. For example, if a recession hits the United States particularly hard, you may be able to mitigate some of the impact by having investments in other regions such as Europe or Asia.

Exposure to Different Currencies:
Investing in different regions can also expose you to

different currencies, which can provide benefits in a recession. For example, if the U.S. dollar depreciates during a recession, investments in other currencies may hold their value better. This can help protect your investments from currency fluctuations and inflation.

Access to Different Markets:
By investing in different regions, you can also gain exposure to different markets and industries. This can help you take advantage of growth opportunities in areas that are not impacted by a recession. For example, during a recession in the United States, you may find growth opportunities in emerging markets such as China or India.

Long-Term Growth Potential:
Finally, geographic diversification can help you achieve long-term growth potential by investing in regions that have different economic cycles and growth rates. By investing in a diverse range of regions, you can spread your investments across different stages of the economic cycle, which can help mitigate risk and increase your chances of achieving long-term growth.

It's important to note that geographic diversification does not guarantee profits or protect against losses in a recession. However, by spreading your investments across different regions, you can reduce risk and increase your chances of achieving long-term growth.

4.4. Use a mix of active and passive investments:
Active and passive investments are two approaches to investing in financial markets. In simple terms, an active

investment strategy involves actively researching, selecting, and managing individual securities with the aim of outperforming the market, while a passive investment strategy involves buying a diversified portfolio of securities that aims to track a market index. Here's a more detailed explanation of each:

Active Investments:

An active investment strategy involves choosing individual stocks, bonds, or other securities, with the goal of beating the market. Active investors often rely on fundamental analysis, which involves analyzing a company's financial statements, management team, and industry trends to identify undervalued stocks or sectors that may perform well in the future. Active investors may also use technical analysis, which involves analyzing charts and historical price data to identify patterns and trends that may signal buying or selling opportunities.

The benefits of an active investment strategy include the potential for higher returns than passive investing, as well as the ability to adjust your portfolio to changing market conditions. However, active investing also involves higher costs, including research expenses and higher trading fees.

Passive Investments:

A passive investment strategy involves buying a diversified portfolio of securities that aims to track a market index, such as the S&P 500 or the Dow Jones Industrial Average. This can be done through an index mutual fund or an exchange-traded fund (ETF). The idea behind passive investing is that it is difficult to consistently outperform the market over the long term, so by investing in a broad index, you can capture the overall performance of the market.

The benefits of a passive investment strategy include lower costs than active investing, since there is no need for expensive research or frequent trading, as well as greater diversification, which can help reduce overall risk. However, passive investing also means you are subject to the ups and downs of the overall market, so you may experience losses during market downturns.

Mixing Active and Passive Investments During a Recession:

During a recession, it can be wise to have a mix of active and passive investments in your portfolio. This is because a recession can create both risks and opportunities in the market. Active investments can help you take advantage of opportunities by identifying undervalued stocks or sectors that may perform well during the downturn. At the same time, passive investments can provide stability and diversification, helping to reduce overall risk.

Starting an Active or Passive Investment Strategy:

If you're interested in starting an active or passive investment strategy, the first step is to determine your investment goals and risk tolerance. Active investing is generally more suitable for investors who are comfortable taking on higher levels of risk in exchange for potentially higher returns, while passive investing is generally more suitable for investors who want to minimize risk and are satisfied with market-level returns.

Ultimately, the best investment strategy will depend on your individual goals, risk tolerance, and financial situation. It's always a good idea to consult with a financial advisor before making any investment decisions.

4.5. Rebalance your portfolio regularly:
Finally, it's important to rebalance your portfolio regularly to maintain your desired asset allocation. During a recession, some asset classes may perform better than others, which can throw off your desired asset allocation. By rebalancing your portfolio regularly, you can ensure that your investments remain properly diversified and aligned with your long-term investment goals.

In summary, investment diversification is an important strategy for investors during a recession. By spreading your investments across different asset classes, industries, and geographies, using a mix of active and passive investments, and rebalancing your portfolio regularly, you can help mitigate risk and protect your portfolio during periods of economic uncertainty.

CHAPTER 5. DON'T PANIC

During a recession, it's natural to feel anxious and uncertain about your investments. However, it's important not to panic and make emotional investment decisions that could harm your long-term financial goals. Here are some key things to keep in mind to avoid panicking with your investments during a recession.

5.1. Focus on your long-term goals:
During a recession, it's easy to get caught up in short-term market fluctuations. However, it's important to remember that investing is a long-term game. By focusing on your long-term investment goals, you can avoid making emotional decisions based on short-term market movements.

5.2. Stay disciplined:
Discipline is key when it comes to investing during a recession. Stick to your investment plan and avoid making impulsive investment decisions. Don't try to time the market or chase hot stocks. Instead, focus on quality investments that align with your long-term investment goals.

5.3. Remember the benefits of diversification:
Diversification is a key strategy for reducing risk in your investment portfolio. By spreading your investments across different asset classes, industries, and geographies, you can reduce the impact of any one investment on your overall portfolio. Remember that a

diversified portfolio may experience less volatility during a recession than a concentrated portfolio.

5.4. Don't try to predict the market:
It's impossible to predict how the stock market will perform during a recession. Instead of trying to time the market or make predictions about the future, focus on your long-term investment goals and stick to your investment plan.

5.5. Seek professional advice:
If you're feeling uncertain about your investments during a recession, consider seeking professional advice from a financial advisor. A financial advisor can provide objective advice and help you make informed decisions about your investments.

In summary, it's important not to panic with your investments during a recession. By focusing on your long-term goals, staying disciplined, remembering the benefits of diversification, not trying to predict the market, and seeking professional advice, you can avoid making emotional investment decisions that could harm your long-term financial goals.

CHAPTER 6. THE PROFESSIONALS

During a recession, it's crucial to seek professional investment advice to help you navigate the market turbulence. Here are some tips to help you find the right professional investment advice during a recession:

6.1. Look for a qualified and experienced financial advisor:
When looking for a financial advisor, make sure they have the necessary qualifications and experience to provide sound investment advice. Look for advisors with certifications such as Certified Financial Planner (CFP) or Chartered Financial Analyst (CFA), and check their experience working in investment management during a recession.

6.2. Consider their investment philosophy:
It's important to find an advisor whose investment philosophy aligns with your goals and risk tolerance. Do they recommend passive or active investment strategies? Are they more focused on growth or income? Understanding their investment philosophy can help you determine whether they're the right fit for you.

6.3. Ask for references and check their track record:
Before hiring a financial advisor, ask for references and check their track record during recessions. Have they successfully navigated previous economic downturns?

Do they have experience managing investment portfolios during turbulent times?

6.4. Understand their fees and compensation structure:

Make sure you understand how your financial advisor is compensated. Are they fee-based or commission-based? Do they receive incentives for recommending certain investments? Understanding their fees and compensation structure can help you avoid conflicts of interest and ensure they're working in your best interest.

6.5. Communicate openly and regularly:

Once you've hired a financial advisor, make sure you communicate openly and regularly. Keep them informed about your investment goals, risk tolerance, and any changes in your financial situation. Regular communication can help ensure your investment portfolio is aligned with your goals and risk tolerance.

Seeking professional investment advice during a recession can be an important step in navigating the market turbulence and building a successful investment portfolio. By looking for a qualified and experienced financial advisor whose investment philosophy aligns with your goals and risk tolerance, checking their track record during recessions, understanding their fees and compensation structure, and communicating regularly, you can find the right professional investment advice to help you achieve long-term financial success.

30 FUN FACTS

Here are 30 fun and interesting facts about investments in past recessions:

1. During the Great Recession of 2008-2009, while the stock market was down 57%, the price of gold increased by 25% as investors sought safe haven assets.

2. According to a study by Vanguard, a $10,000 investment in a portfolio of 50% stocks and 50% bonds at the start of the Great Recession would have grown to $22,736 by the end of 2019, even including the downturn.

3. During the Great Depression of the 1930s, the film industry boomed as people sought entertainment and escapism. Box office sales reached record highs during this time.

4. In the early 1980s recession, investor Warren Buffett made a series of strategic investments in companies such as American Express and Coca-Cola, which paid off handsomely in the years following the recession.

5. Following the 2008-2009 recession, the unemployment rate in the U.S. peaked at 10%, but by February 2020, it had fallen to a 50-year low of 3.5%.

6. Despite the economic turmoil of the 2008-2009 recession, some companies saw significant profits,

including Apple, which released the iPhone in 2007 and experienced explosive growth in the following years.

7. The COVID-19 pandemic and resulting recession led to a surge in e-commerce, with online sales in the U.S. increasing by 44% year-over-year in 2020, according to Digital Commerce 360.

8. Some investors made a fortune by buying distressed assets during the Great Recession, including Warren Buffett, who invested $5 billion in Goldman Sachs in 2008 and earned a 43% return on his investment within five years.

9. During the 1980-1982 recession, a group of investors known as the "Boston Chicken Bandits" made a fortune by investing in Boston Chicken (later renamed Boston Market), which went public in 1993 and saw explosive growth in the following years.

10. During the Great Recession, Netflix saw significant growth as people cut back on other forms of entertainment. The company's stock price increased by more than 300% between 2008 and 2010.

11. The COVID-19 pandemic led to a surge in demand for home renovation and DIY projects, with Home Depot reporting record sales in 2020.

12. In the 1970s recession, oil prices spiked due to geopolitical tensions in the Middle East, leading to significant profits for oil companies.

13. Some investors made a fortune by investing in distressed real estate assets during the Great Recession, including billionaire Sam Zell, who purchased a portfolio of distressed properties for $39 billion in 2007 and saw significant returns in the years following the recession.

14. During the 2008-2009 recession, Goldman Sachs made billions of dollars by betting against the subprime mortgage market.

15. The COVID-19 pandemic led to a surge in demand for technology stocks, with companies such as Amazon, Apple, and Microsoft seeing significant growth in their stock prices.

16. In the 2000-2001 recession, some investors made a fortune by investing in tech companies such as Google, which went public in 2004 and saw significant growth in the following years.

17. Following the 1987 stock market crash, some investors saw significant profits by investing in undervalued stocks that had been oversold.

18. During the Great Recession, some investors made a fortune by investing in distressed debt assets, including private equity firms such as Blackstone and Apollo Global Management.

19. During the 1970s recession, Hershey's saw significant growth as people turned to affordable indulgences. The company's profits increased by 57% in

1974.

20. The COVID-19 pandemic led to a surge in demand for streaming services, with Disney+ gaining 73 million subscribers in its first year.

21. During the 2008-2009 recession, some investors made a fortune by investing in healthcare stocks, including companies such as Johnson & Johnson and Pfizer.

22. Following the 2008-2009 recession, some investors saw significant profits by investing in emerging markets, including countries such as China and India.

23. The 1980-1982 recession saw a surge in demand for discount retailers, including Walmart, which saw significant growth in the following years.

24. During the Great Recession, General Electric (GE) saw significant profits from its financial arm, GE Capital, which focused on consumer lending and credit cards.

25. The COVID-19 pandemic led to a surge in demand for home fitness equipment, with Peloton reporting record sales in 2020.

26. In the 1970s recession, tobacco stocks such as Philip Morris saw significant growth as people turned to vices for comfort.

27. During the Great Recession, some investors made a fortune by investing in distressed municipal bonds,

including those issued by the city of Detroit.

28. The 2000-2001 recession saw a surge in demand for online advertising, leading to significant growth for companies such as Google and Yahoo.

29. During the COVID-19 pandemic, the stock price of video conferencing company Zoom increased by more than 500%, as people turned to remote work and virtual meetings.

30. Following the 1987 stock market crash, some investors saw significant profits by investing in safe haven assets such as gold and treasury bonds.

EPILOGUE

Investing during a recession can be a daunting task, but it's also an opportunity to build a strong, diversified investment portfolio that can weather economic storms. Throughout this book, we've explored various investment strategies that can help you navigate a recession and build a successful investment portfolio.

We've discussed the importance of having an emergency fund, investing in quality companies, diversifying your investments, and staying disciplined during market downturns. We've also talked about the benefits of dollar-cost averaging, seeking professional advice, and not panicking with your investments.

While investing during a recession can be challenging, it's important to remember that recessions are a normal part of the economic cycle. They may be difficult to predict, but they are inevitable.

Investing during a recession requires patience, discipline, and a willingness to take calculated risks. But it also provides opportunities for growth and diversification that may not be available during more stable economic times.

As we close this book, I encourage you to continue learning about investing, staying disciplined, and seeking professional advice when necessary. With these tools and a long-term investment mindset, you can navigate a recession and build a successful investment portfolio that can provide long-term financial security.

APPS & RESOURCES
There are many apps and resources available to help with investing during a recession. Here are some popular options:

1. Robinhood: Robinhood is a commission-free trading app that allows you to buy and sell stocks, options, and cryptocurrencies. It also provides real-time market data and news.

2. Acorns: Acorns is an investment app that helps you invest your spare change automatically. It rounds up your purchases to the nearest dollar and invests the difference in a diversified portfolio of stocks and bonds.

3. Personal Capital: Personal Capital is an online wealth management platform that offers investment management, retirement planning, and financial advisory services. It also provides tools to help you track your net worth and investment performance.

4. Yahoo Finance: Yahoo Finance is a comprehensive financial news and analysis website that offers real-time stock quotes, financial news, and market data.

5. Investopedia: Investopedia is a popular online resource for investing and personal finance education. It provides articles, videos, tutorials, and a dictionary of financial terms.

6. Morningstar: Morningstar is a leading investment

research firm that offers analysis, ratings, and data on stocks, mutual funds, and exchange-traded funds (ETFs).

7. Bloomberg: Bloomberg is a financial news and data provider that offers real-time market data, news, and analysis on stocks, bonds, currencies, and commodities.

GLOSSARY OF INVESTMENT TERMS

Absolute Return Fund: see Hedge Fund.

Active Management: a form of investment management that involves buying and selling financial assets with the objective of earning returns greater than a specified benchmark.

Active Management Return: the difference between a portfolio's return and the benchmark's return.

Active Management Risk: the risk taken by an active portfolio manager to earn active management returns by taking positions different from the benchmark; typically measured by the standard deviation of active management returns.

Actuary: a person or firm that specializes in estimating the liabilities associated with a benefit plan or an insurance trust.

Agency Conflict: the potential for conflict of interest between an agent and the person or organization for which the agent is acting.

Alternative Investment: a term used to categorize assets other than traditional publicly traded stocks and bonds, including but not limited to private equity, real estate, hedge funds, commodities, timber, and infrastructure.

Asset Allocation: the process of determining the desired

division of an investor's portfolio among available asset classes.
Asset Class: a broadly defined generic group of financial assets, such as stocks or bonds.

Benchmark: a portfolio with which the investment performance of an investor can be compared for the purpose of determining investment skill. A benchmark portfolio represents a relevant and investable alternative to the investor's actual portfolio and, in particular, is similar in terms of risk exposure.

Benefits: periodic payments promised or expected to be made to the designated beneficiaries of a pool of assets.

Benefit Security Ratio: see Funded Ratio.

Bond (also Fixed-Income Security): a type of investment in which the holder lends money to another entity and is then entitled to periodic payments of interest and a return of the capital at a specified time in the future.

Buyout: a form of private equity in which a partnership buys all the shares of a public company, usually taking on a large debt, to operate the company privately with the intention of eventually making a profit by taking the company public again or selling part or all of it to another business.

Commingled Fund: an investment vehicle that sells units of ownership in itself to one or more investors and uses the proceeds to purchase financial assets for the benefit of the investors. The investors have a pro rata claim on the assets of the fund proportional to their unit ownership.

Common Stock (also Equity; Stock): legal representations of an ownership position in a corporation.

Commodity: a physical (real) asset used as an input to a production process. Many commodities are traded in cash (spot) markets or on organized exchanges in the form of futures contracts.

Conflict of Interest: a situation in which a person who has a duty to one party acts in such a way as to benefit the person (or a related party) at the expense of the party to whom the duty is owed.

Contributions: money added to a pool of assets for the purpose of investment and, eventually, payment of benefits.

Correlation: a statistical measure of the co-variation of two random variables (i.e., how much two variables change together).

Custodian Bank: a type of bank that provides safekeeping of financial securities for an investor, including the related accounting and reporting services.

Defined-Benefit Plan: a retirement plan in which the participants are promised a fixed benefit. The sponsoring organization takes the risk that its investments will be sufficient to provide these benefits.

Defined-Contribution Plan: a retirement plan in which a participant (and perhaps a sponsoring organization) makes fixed contributions and the participant bears the risk that the assets will be sufficient to provide adequate benefits upon retirement.

Diversification: the process of investing in more than one type of asset to reduce the risk of the entire portfolio.

Endowment: a gift, usually to an educational institution, whose purpose is to provide funding for a particular mission in perpetuity. Collectively, an aggregate of such gifts being managed in a single strategy.

Equity: see Common Stock.

Expected Return: the return on a security (or portfolio) that an investor anticipates receiving over a given time horizon.

Fiduciary: a person or entity that assumes responsibility to manage or oversee a pool of assets on behalf of some other person or entity, such as a pension fund or endowment. The fiduciary has a duty to act solely for the benefit of that entity (not himself/herself or some other entity).

Fiduciary Duty: a legal or ethical relationship of confidence or trust between two or more parties.

Financial Asset (also Security): a legal representation of

the right to receive prospective future benefits under stated conditions.

Fixed-Income Security: see Bond.

Foundation: an entity that has some public mission (e.g., to cure a given disease) and provides grants to other entities to further that mission (e.g., by conducting scientific research to find a cure). It owns a pool of assets that are invested to provide income to fund that mission.

Funded Ratio (also Benefit Security Ratio): the ratio of the value of a fund's assets to the value of the fund's liabilities.

General Partner: an individual or firm that sources and obtains financing for the purchase of an asset and then manages that asset on behalf of other providers of capital (the limited partners).

Governance Structure: the set of processes by which a fund is managed for the benefit of some group of beneficiaries.

Growth Stocks: a segment of an equity market characterized by the stocks of companies that have experienced or are expected to experience earnings per share growth higher than the market as a whole. They also tend to display high price-to-earnings ratios relative to the market. Also called "glamour stocks."

Hedge Fund: a form of active management

distinguished by a lack of traditional guidelines or benchmarks; a hedge fund typically uses derivatives, leverage, and/or short selling. The term is often synonymous with absolute return fund.

Indexing: see Passive Management.

Information Ratio: a risk-adjusted measure of portfolio active management performance. Mathematically, over an evaluation period, it is the annualized ratio of active management return to active management risk, where risk is measured by the standard deviation of the portfolio's active management returns.

Investable Universe: the aggregate of securities that is appropriate and available for selection under a particular investment mandate.

Investment Committee: a group of individuals who are responsible for determining the investment policy of a fund.

Investment Consultant: a professional (usually associated with a firm) who offers advisory services to a fund, most often in the areas of asset allocation, investment policy and manager selection.

Investment Manager: a person or entity that creates and manages portfolios of
securities for clients with money to invest.

Investment Policy: a component of the investment process that involves determining a fund's mission, objectives, and attitude toward the trade-off between expected return and risk.

Investment Policy Statement: a formal written document describing a fund's investment policy.

Investment Return: the percentage change in the value of an investment in a financial asset (or portfolio of financial assets) over a specified time period.

Investment Risk: the potential for loss accepted by an investor in the pursuit of investment return; alternatively, the uncertainty associated with the end-of-period value of an investment.

Investment Skill: the ability of an active manager to select portfolios that consistently have average returns greater than a given performance benchmark.

Liability: the present value of the accrued benefits promised to the beneficiaries of a fund.

Limited Partner: an individual or entity that provides equity financing to a general partner for the purchase of an investment but does not participate in the ongoing management of the investment.

Liquidity: property of a security that allows investors to convert the security to cash at a price similar to the price of the previous trade in the security (assuming that no significant new information has arrived since the previous trade).

Mandate: the strategy or performance benchmark used by an investment manager on behalf of and at the direction of a client.

Market Capitalization: the aggregate market value of a security, equal to the market price per unit of the security multiplied by the total number of outstanding units of the security.

Market Cycle: a period of time over which a particular security market moves from one peak to another or one trough to another.

Market Index: a collection of securities whose values are averaged to reflect the overall investment performance of a particular market for financial assets.

Money-Weighted Rate of Return: the rate of return on a portfolio over a particular period of time. It is the discount rate that makes the present value of cash flows into and out of the portfolio, as well as the portfolio's ending value, equal to the portfolio's beginning value.

Mutual Fund: a managed investment company, with an unlimited life, that stands ready at all times to purchase its shares from its owners and usually will continuously offer new shares to the public.

Overfunded: the status of a fund whose assets are greater in value than the associated plan's liabilities.

Passive Management (also Indexing): the process of buying and holding a well-diversified portfolio designed to produce substantially the same returns as a specified market index.

Peer Group: a set of investors (funds or managers) whose returns are used for a comparison with those of a given fund to determine how the given fund ranks among similar funds.

Performance Appraisal: the part of the performance evaluation process that attempts to determine whether the investment returns over an evaluation period have been achieved by skill or luck.

Performance Attribution: the part of the performance evaluation process that identifies sources of returns for a portfolio relative to a designated benchmark over an evaluation period.

Performance Evaluation: a component of the investment process involving periodic analysis of how a portfolio performed in terms of both returns earned and risks incurred.

Performance Measurement: the part of the performance evaluation process that calculates a portfolio's rate of return over an evaluation period.

Plan Participant: a member of a defined-benefit or defined-contribution plan to whom benefits are promised or are being paid.

Policy Asset Mix: a set of asset classes and desired percentage allocations to each such that the total portfolio displays the investor's desired risk and expected return profile; also referred to as the "policy portfolio," "policy benchmark," "policy asset allocation," or "strategic asset allocation."

Private Equity: a broad asset class generally involving buyouts, venture capital, and distressed debt converted to equity.

Real Estate: an investment in land and physical structures intended to provide a stream of rental or lease income and possibly capital appreciation.

Rebalancing: the process of buying and selling assets to restore a fund to its policy asset mix after market movements or net cash flows have changed the actual market weights of the various asset classes.

Relative Performance: the difference between a portfolio's return and the benchmark's return.

Risk Budgeting: a risk management technique in which assets are allocated efficiently so that the expected return of each asset is proportional to its contribution to portfolio risk.

Risk Management: a part of the investment process in which the risks of a portfolio are identified and quantified; then, strategies are developed to control those risks.

Risk Tolerance: the trade-off between risk and expected return demanded by a particular investor.

Scenario Analysis: a process whereby, for the purpose of designing appropriate investment strategies, an investor considers a number of possible future economic investment environments and the likelihood of those environments occurring.

Security: see Financial Asset.

Separately Managed Account: an investment vehicle that takes in funds from a single investor and uses the proceeds to purchase financial assets for the sole benefit of that investor. The investor directly owns all assets held in the account. Also called "separate account."

Sharpe Ratio: a risk-adjusted measure of portfolio performance in which risk is measured by the standard deviation of the portfolio's returns. Mathematically, over an evaluation period, it is the annualized ratio of excess return (actual return less the risk-free return) of the portfolio divided by the portfolio's standard deviation.

Staff: the professionals who, on a day-to-day basis, administer the investment program of a fund.

Standard Deviation: a statistical measure of the variability (range of potential outcomes) of investment returns.

Stock: see Common Stock.

Stress Test: a form of analysis in which one estimates

the impact of various adverse situations on the returns of a portfolio.

Taft–Hartley fund: a multi-employer defined-benefit plan whose beneficiaries are members of a labor union with members working for multiple employers.

Time-Weighted Rate of Return: the rate of return on a portfolio over a particular period of time. Effectively, it is the return on $1.00 invested in the portfolio at the beginning of the measurement period.

Trustee: a person who has fiduciary responsibility for a pool of assets.

Uncertainty: the state of incomplete knowledge about the present and future with respect to an investment.

Uncorrelated: condition in which the returns of two or more assets do not go in the same direction at the same time.

Underfunded: the status of a fund whose assets are less in value than the liabilities for which those assets exist.

Value Stocks: a segment of an equity market characterized by the stocks of companies that have experienced poor past price performance or whose issuing companies have experienced relatively poor past earnings compared with the market as a whole. They tend to display low price-to-earnings ratios relative to the market. Also called "distressed stocks."

Venture Capital: a form of private equity involving non-publicly traded equity investments in which a general partner provides capital to an entrepreneur to begin or grow an enterprise with the intention of eventually making a profit by taking the company public or selling it to another business.

Volatility: the characteristic that financial asset returns vary over time in unpredictable ways or amounts. This term is often used interchangeably with the standard deviation of the asset's returns.